ANYONE Can Invest in Real Estate

Complete Real Estate Investing Guide

BY: Matthew E Hamm

Copyright © 2018 by Matthew E Hamm

All rights reserved. No part of this book may be reproduced in any form on or by an electronic or mechanical means, including information storage and retrieval systems, without permission in writing from the publisher, except by a reviewer who may quote brief passages in a review.

The advice and strategies found within may not be suitable for every situation. This work is sold with the understanding that neither the author nor the publisher are held responsible for the results accrued from the advice in this book.

REinvestWise.com

Contents

Introduction

Anyone CAN Invest in Real Estate

Where to Start: Financing a Purchase

Rentals

Fix n' Flips

Make a business Plan

Why You Should Become a Realtor

Keep Moving Forward

Introduction

This book is a complete guide on how to start investing in real estate. You will find this guide helpful whether you are a beginner or not and as you will see in the first chapter **Anyone CAN Invest in Real Estate.**

Before I get in too deep, I want to tell you a little about myself and my experiences.

I am a Realtor with Nova Star Real Estate. I currently manage the Massillon Ohio branch of the company. I work with Buyers, Sellers and Investors. I serve clients in the Residential and Commercial markets.

Before I obtained my real estate salesperson license, I was a home Inspector. I got my education for home inspection and real estate from Hondros College. This is a great school choice for the real estate industry because of their high success rate.

I was a home inspector for about two years before I received my real estate salesperson license. I continued to inspect houses for a couple years after this but then I decided to hang up the inspector career to focus more on real estate sales and investing.

I started out investing in real estate without any guidance or education in this specific area. I tried to get into real estate investing once before I became a Realtor, but it did not work out. I was working with an agent that claimed to have knowledge in this area but that agent lead me down a bunch of dead ends. After wasting much time and energy we mutually parted ways.

Moving forward, now that I had my own license I could look at properties any time I wanted. I looked at a few and finally bought one. Again, I had no guidance and the purchase wasn't horrible, but it wasn't what I planned. I highly recommend getting some training, guidance or at least find a good Realtor with investment property experience of his own (not just selling investment properties but owning them as well).

After a few years of figuring things out on my own the hard way, I eventually became successful and produced some profits. I now own a few rentals, I have flipped a couple houses and I have owned multiunit commercial property.

Looking back on my own experiences I realized how much easier things could have been if I had someone to help me and guide me. I could have made more money and built a bigger portfolio. This has allowed me to realize the need that new or aspiring investors have, that is Guidance.

This book and my **"Real Estate Investing Beginners Guide Program"** are the result of this need. I hope that you find it helpful and I know it will help you be more profitable!

Chapter One

Anyone CAN Invest in Real Estate

It is true, anyone CAN invest in Real Estate but not everyone will be great at it. I will show you how anyone can become a real estate investor but again not everyone should do it.

Real estate investing is a career choice and just like every other career out there some people will be good, others will be great, but some will just be terrible at it. Some of the key traits of a great real estate investor are Budgeting, Organization and Scheduling. Even if you are not great at these yet, as long as you want to be good at them and put the effort in then you will be fine.

How Is It Possible That ANYONE Can Be A Real Estate Investor?

Simply because no matter how much money you currently have, or how much experience you have in real estate you can still get started. You don't have to be an expert or rich to get started.

While it may be easier for you if you are sitting on $100,000 and years of experience but the truth is that most real estate investors start off with no experience and very little money.

In the next chapter I will discuss in detail how to start investing with little or no money, so right now I'm going to focus on...

How to Get Started with Little or No Experience?

The First Step:

Honestly you are already doing the right thing, researching and educating yourself.

Looking up and reading books and articles written by experienced real estate investors is the best way to get started. It will get you familiar with ideas and terms involved. I have plenty of articles on my website REinvestWise.com that will help you learn more.

Have you heard the term "Education is the key to success"? This is true in real estate investing as well as many other things in life. The more you know when starting out the more successful you will be in your investing career.

One advantage of reading articles from other investors is that you get the benefit of learning from their mistakes without having to lose any of your own money. The best part about making a mistake is that it shows you one way to not do something. The best part about learning from someone else's mistakes is that you lost nothing while learning a lesson.

This brings us to...

The Second Step:

Learn from someone who has been investing in real estate for five plus years.

You need to create a foundation of real estate investing knowledge by doing your own research and educating yourself. Once you have created this foundation you need to find a way to build on it. You can either start on your own and hope for the best or you can find someone with real life experience that you can learn from.

I went with the first option, I learned a little and then started out on my own. I could have had more help if I would have asked for it. I knew a couple real estate investors, but I didn't want to bother them. I figured I would be fine, and I would learn as I go. I did learn from all the mistakes I made, and I did ok, but it could have been much better.

If you know someone that is a real estate investor, I suggest that you sit down with them and start asking questions. I am sure they will be willing to at least do that. If you are lucky, they may be willing to take you under their wing and show you the ropes. That would be the best-case scenario.

If you don't know any investors or you can't get any one to sit and talk with you the next best thing would be to find one online and talk with them. Obviously, you need to check out the possible consultant to make sure they are legitimate. Check their current employment situation to make sure they are still active in the real estate investment market. You should also check how long they have been successfully investing in real estate. I suggest an approximant time of a minimum of five years.

I offer a consulting program. If you are interested check out **REinvestWise.com/Resources.** I have programs that will fit all your needs no matter where you are in your investing career. I have Email Correspondence or Phone Consulting programs that will fit any budget. Check it out, I would be happy to work with you.

Chapter Two

Where to Start: Financing a Purchase

Now that you have built a foundation of knowledge and you have learned from an experienced real estate investor it is time to get the ball rolling.

There are so many ways to finance a real estate investment purchase. None of them are necessarily right or wrong and not everyone should go down the same path. Some options are better than others and I will go over a few of them with you and try to help you make the right choice.

The Four Most Common Real Estate Investment Financing Options

Cash Purchases, Equity Lines, Personal Loans, Conventional Loans. Investors use a variety of these all the time and they are all great options except for Personal Loans. This is for two reasons, Higher Interest Rates and Lower Caps. We will go over all of this.

Cash Purchases

The term "Cash is King" rings true in the real estate investing market. This is by far the best option for financing your investment purchases but believe it or not it may not be the best option for you.

The number one reason cash purchases are a great way to go is that there is no interest to pay. That means more of your money stays in your pocket. Interest rates flow with the market and right now they are up and going to continue to climb during the near future.

If you can purchase with cash and save the interest payments that's great. You can save anywhere from 5-12%. Let's say you purchase a property for $35,000 and you put $15,000 into it. If you take out a loan to finance this, you will end up paying around $218 a month in interest or $2,600 a year.

Assuming a $50,000 single family home would bring in $700 per month in rent you would net $8,400 per year, subtract the $2,600 in interest and your income goes down to $5,800.

We can estimate the rest of your expenses to figure out how much your profit from this property. Yearly taxes in my area for this home would be around $950, insurance would be $700, in my area the owner pays the sewer bill which is about $280 a year. You will probably have a random repair here and there so, let's add another $500 in repairs. This brings your profit down to $3,370. Remember that's with the interest payments added in. If you paid cash for this investment your profit jumps up to $5,970. That's a big difference! Especially if you multiply that by 10 or 15 properties.

I know what you're thinking... $500 in repairs??? Well imagine the water heater goes out, to have a plumber install a new one will cost $800-$1,400 in my area. So, with one repair you already passed your budgeted repair allowance. Now the water heater may not go out every year, well I hope not, but there are so many things that come up during the year and it all eats into your profits.

Maybe you don't have any cash laying around? Well, Good News! There are benefits to using loans and I will get into that soon, so don't worry if you're not rich or you haven't saved up $50,000. You can still invest in real estate even if you don't have any money in your savings account.

Equity Lines

If you have done some research on real estate investing, then I'm sure you have seen the term **HELOC**. This stands for **Home Equity Line Of Credit**. It is simply an Equity Loan.

Equity Loans are a very popular way to purchase investment properties. This is how I financed my first investment property. At the time an Equity Loan was my only option. I had less then $1,000 in savings but I had around $40,000 in equity in my home. So, I took out a HELOC and bought my first investment property.

When using a HELOC to purchase a property you can purchase as a CASH purchase. This is because your financing is not connected to the property you are purchasing, it is connected to a property you already own. The benefit to purchase as a CASH purchase is that it gives you buying power.

Sellers love cash offers. They can close faster, there is no appraisal or FHA Inspections. You can usually get a better deal on a property when purchasing CASH.

How do HELOCs Work

If you don't know how HELOCs work don't worry they are not that complicated. It is simply a loan to borrow the difference of what you owe for a property from 85% of the Market Value.

First, you must have a piece of property in your name. This doesn't mean that you must own it out right you just have to have legal title to the property. Most investors that use HELOCs have a mortgage on their home and then get the HELOC on top. The original mortgage becomes the first mortgage and the HELOC takes second place.

Depending on the lender you use you can take up to 85% of the value of your home. Let's say your home is worth $100,000 then you could take up to $85,000 against your home. If you owe $50,000 on your original mortgage, then you could take up to $35,000 on a HELOC.

You can also take out HELOCs on your investment properties. I have done this to help fund more investment properties. I will get into this in more detail in the chapter **"Make a Business Plan"**.

Once you go to your lender and open the line of credit (The HELOC) you don't have to take that money out until needed. That is the difference between a loan and line of credit. With a HELOC you will have the funds available to you whenever you need it whether for a purchase or repairs on an investment, so only take out what you need when you need it so that you don't have to pay interest on money that you haven't used yet.

Personal Loans

This is my least favorite type of financing for investment properties. The biggest reason is the higher interest rates. The higher your interest rate is the lower your profits will be.

There are two main types of personal loans, secured and unsecured. A secured loan is when you take something of value (like a car) and put a lien against it (for the amount of the loan). You will get a lower interest rate by doing this, but you may not be able to borrow much unless you own very valuable things that you have paid off.

An unsecured loan has nothing of value attached to it. Therefore, the interest rate goes up. It becomes more of a risk for the lender to give you money with nothing of value attached to it. If you stop paying on the loan they have nothing to repo to get their money back.

Many lenders have stopped offering unsecured loans and the ones that do only allow up to around $5,000 and you can't buy any property that you plan to make money on with $5,000. If you want to use unsecured loans you might have to find private lenders that still offer these but be ready to pay over 10% in interest.

Personal loans can also be taken out from your credit card accounts. This is a form of "Hard Money Loans". Doing this is a huge risk with the outrageous interest rates that credit companies carry. This should be considered a last resort but for me it is never an option. I have seen once or twice where a house flipper used this type of funding to help finish a remodel and it turned out ok because it was a very short-term loan. They didn't profit as much due to the higher interest they paid though.

My advice on personal loans is to be very careful and honestly you should try to avoid this type of financing.

Conventional Loans

This is a much better option then personal loans because it will have a much lower interest rate due to it being attached to the actual investment property you are purchasing.

The biggest "Pros" of conventional loans is the lower interest rate, (which means more profit) and the structured payment plan. It is common for a conventional loan on an investment property to be a 20-

year term. This means you can build a business plan around the payoff dates of your long-term investments.

Your payments will include interest and principal, this allows you to pay it down and pay it off. HELOCs are usually interest only and you can fall into the trap of never paying them off by only making the minimum interest only payments.

The two biggest "Cons" are restrictions on the property's condition and you will max out your debt to income ratio at some point. It doesn't matter too much which financing route you take at some point you will max out your debt to income ratio. There are ways to extend your buying ability and purchase more properties before hitting the max debt to income ratio, but I will get into that in more detail in the chapter **"Make a Business Plan".**

The other problem with conventional loans is that they put restrictions on the property concerning condition and value. This means that they will send an appraiser out to look at the property and two bad things could happen. The appraiser could say that the property isn't worth enough to give you the loan on it or the property is in disrepair.

The lender will only lend up to 80% of the value of the property. This means the property must appraise for 20% higher then the purchase price minus the down payment. In a Hot market when property values are up this usually is not a problem. It becomes more of a problem when property values go down.

If you want to buy an investment property for $35,000 with a 10% down Conventional loan you will need it to appraise for $39,375 or higher. To figure this out you must subtract your down payment from the purchase price then divide by 80%.

Example:

$35,000	Purchase Price
-$3,500	10% Down Payment
$31,500	This is 80% of the value needed
÷0.80	80%
$39,375	Appraised Value Needed for a $35,000 Purchase Price

Don't worry if this doesn't make much sense to you or you can't remember this formula next time you look at a property. You don't have to do this yourself. Your Realtor can do this for you.

When your lender sends out the appraiser, he is not just looking for the value of the home, he is also looking at the condition. He won't be looking at the wallpaper or paint colors. He is going to be looking for the "big stuff" like foundation, broken windows, age of roof.

Usually when you are looking at an investment property it is going to have some needed repairs. That's why you can get a better deal on it. You just need to make sure there are no major repairs needed.

How do I Know Which Type of Financing to Use?

I find that for most people there really is no option. Most people don't have all of these options available so their path to purchasing real estate investments is already chosen for them.

This is always a case by case situation. If you have $100,000 in savings, then you would be best off to go in all cash. When the money runs out you can start using loans.

If you only have $1,000 in cash, then you will want to get an equity loan for the down payment and then use conventional loans for the purchases.

If you have $10,000 to $30,000 in savings, then you can skip the equity loan and go with conventional loan purchases and pay cash for the down payments.

You can see there are options to financing an investment property. If you try hard enough, you can find a way.

Chapter Three

Rentals

When it comes to real estate investing there are many options. I want to focus on two of the most common choices, Rentals and Fix n' Flips. The next chapter will be about Fix n' Flips, for this chapter I will be focusing on Rental Properties.

Rental properties are a very good option for long term investing. There actually is a way to create short term investments with rentals by using Lease Options but I'll get to that later.

In this chapter we will go over **How to Find a Good Rental Property, How to Set a Rehab Budget, How to Find a Good Tenant** and **How to be a Successful Landlord.**

By the end of this chapter you will have the information you need to be a great landlord. You will be ready to start your successful investing career

How to Find a Good Rental Property

There are many ways to find a good rental property. The best option is to hook up with a good local Realtor, but not just any Realtor you need to find one that is an expert in investment properties. This will be someone that personally owns a few rental properties, single family, multifamily and commercial properties. You could go with a Realtor that has sold these types of properties, but they will not have the experience needed to help you when you are just starting out.

Once you find a good local Realtor that is an expert in investment properties you will need to decide what type of property you want to start your investing career with. If you picked the right Realtor, they will be able to help you make this decision rather quickly.

To help you make this decision I have written an article "Real Estate Investing: Single Family or Multifamily" on my website REinvestWise.com I have included it here to show you the benefits of owning each type of property.

Benefits to Owning Single Family Properties

Less Expenses

When it comes to renting single family homes, one of the benefits is that all the utilities are in the tenant's name and they pay for them. It's one less thing for you, the owner, to have to deal with. It's also one less expense to take away from your monthly rental profit.

Some multifamily properties have the utilities split but, in my area, Northeastern Ohio, most multifamily properties have one or more utilities that are not separated, and the owner must pay this bill. Yes, you can charge more rent to try to make up for it, but you are at the mercy of the tenant for their usage of that utility. Personally, I don't like to buy any property that leaves me paying the bills for the tenants.

Less Time Involved

Now this really depends on the tenant you have and the condition of the property. In general, most single-family homes bring you a steady stream of income monthly and all you have to do is take the check to the bank. I always write the lease agreement up so that the tenant is responsible for lawn maintenance and snow removal, this way I don't have to waste an evening mowing the grass for my rental property.

You will still want to do a drive by of your properties every month or so. I even schedule a quarterly walkthrough inspection of my rentals just to make sure everything is in good working condition.

Longer Terms

I find that most of my single-family homes have a lower vacancy rate then multi family. If your property is in good condition, a decent sized home and your rent is set correctly then your tenants will want to stay for a long time.

Multifamily properties usually have smaller room sizes, tenants must share the outdoor spaces and their neighbors are just a little too close. They are either just on the other side of the wall in a side by side or right upstairs in an up and down unit. These reasons tend to cause tenants to look for a better situation and you end up with a higher vacancy rate.

Lease Option Possibilities

A definition is… A lease for a specific term limit with the option for the tenant to purchase the property written into the lease.

There are many benefits to the tenant to do this, one would be they can allocate part of their rent payment toward the principal balance during the lease term.

I don't want to spend too much time on the tenants benefits though, I want to focus on the benefits for the owner.

The biggest benefit is the extra cash flow. On a lease option the tenant pays a fee upfront to have the right to purchase the property. This comes off the purchase price if/when the tenant buys the property but, if the tenant does not buy the property then the money is forfeited to the owner. If the tenant wants, they can pay down their purchase price with additional monthly payments.

So, you have a single-family home that rents for $600 per month. That's $14,400 gross income for 2 years. Take that same property and do a lease option with it… the number gets better. Instead of $600 per month you could get a tenant to pay $600 plus $200 extra per month towards the purchase price and they pay $4,000 upfront for the option. Now we have $23,200 in gross income. Much better right?

You must make sure the purchase price you agree on will work for you if the tenant follows through with the purchase which happens only about half the time.

Benefits of Owning Multifamily Properties

Higher Rent per property

Let's say we have a large 4-bedroom single-family home that was converted into a duplex. As a single-family home, it would bring in $1,000 per month, hypothetically. Now that it's converted into a duplex it has two 2-bedroom apartments that bring in $600 each, that's $1,200 per month. That would be $2,400 more in gross income per year.

Less Time and Money Involved in Purchasing

Every home you purchase involves closing costs. If you purchase with cash your closing costs may only be $1,000-$2,000 per purchase but if you are using some type of financing, you will then have lender fees to pay which could bring your closing costs up to $4,000-$5,000 per purchase. Let's say we want 10 rental units, if we bought all single-family homes with cash it would cost us up to $20,000 in closing costs. If we bought all duplexes with cash, it would cost us up to $10,000. You can save money by buying multifamily properties.

Guaranteed or Forced Appreciation

A single-family home's value will always be dependent on the current market, so if the market is up the value is up, if the market is down the value goes down. Multifamily properties value is calculated differently. The value is determined by the income it brings in. Unlike the market, rent always increases. This means your value on a multifamily will always be slowly increasing.

There are other factors involved in calculating value but to simplify we are assuming that general maintenance has been done to keep the property in good condition.

Lower Financial Risk

Every investment has some risk involved. Any vacancy in a single-family home reduces the income to $0 and leaves you paying the bills. With a multifamily property there is less chance of bringing in $0 per month. On a duplex, if one unit is empty then your income reduces to half, but that half should be enough to carry your expenses on the property or at least close to it.

You now know the benefits of owning single family and multifamily residential properties so let's go over a few benefits of commercial rental properties.

Benefits to Owning Commercial Rental Properties

Commercial properties are quite a bit different from residential properties. Everything from purchasing, renting and selling is different. I won't be spending too much time on commercial properties since it is not likely that you will be starting your investing career with these types of properties. I will give you a few benefits to get you thinking about the future.

Higher Income Potential

Commercial rental space rents for a much higher rate per square foot then residential. In my area commercial property rents for around 35% higher per square foot than residential rental property.

Now commercial property usually costs more to purchase so your initial investment will be higher, but you will produce a higher monthly income from your investment.

Less Risks with Tenants

You will find out when you start screening tenants for your residential rental properties that it is nearly impossible to know if a tenant will be a good or bad tenant. I do all the background and credit checks and I find out that if a potential tenant looks good on paper this doesn't necessarily mean they will turn out to be good tenants.

When you are working with commercial tenants you will find that there is a much lower number of "Bad" tenants. There are a few reasons for this; these tenants have already been screened by lenders and banks for their business accounts and commercial tenants are usually more responsible since they run a profitable business.

Commercial tenants have to be more responsible when it comes to taking care of the property and paying rent on time because they depend on that space to make a living and run their business. They also know that they can be evicted with little or no notice, which is a huge difference from the residential world where it takes forever to evict a bad tenant.

Guaranteed Appreciation

Just like I mentioned in the section about multifamily homes, commercial property value is calculated by the income it produces. A residential property value will always be dependent on the current market, so if the market is up the value is up, if the market is down the value goes down. Commercial property value is calculated differently. The value is determined by the income it brings in. Unlike the market, rent always increases. This means your value on a commercial property will always be slowly increasing.

Now that you know the benefits of owning single-family and multifamily residential homes and commercial rental properties you should be able to sit down and decide which type of property fits you and your needs. After you decide which property type to pursue you now need to start looking.

A few tips to finding the right rental property would be...

1. Use a good local Realtor that is an expert in real estate investing.

2. Find a property that needs a little work done: updating and repairs.
3. Location! Find the worst property on a good street.
4. Be Active! A good deal wont last more than a day or two, watch the market daily.
5. Be ready to put an offer in before you see the property.
6. Write a clean offer. The less you ask for the better price you will get.

How to Set a Rehab Budget

By now you have chosen which type of property to pursue and you have found a great deal with the help of your Realtor. Now you must set a rehab budget, let me give you a few suggestions, from my experience, on how to decide on a rehab budget.

What Dollar Amount Should I Put on my Budget?

This will be a case by case situation. Every property you buy will need different things repaired and updated, so you will need to assess the property before you buy it and decide then what you need to and want to put in the rehab budget.

As a rule of thumb, in my area, investors are aiming to have between $35,000 and $45,000 invested in each unit. Notice I said unit, if you are buying a multifamily property you will be able to invest more then $35,000 and still produce a valuable income property.

I aim for the $35,000 as the maximum investment per unit on my properties. In the current market that is nearly impossible, but I still try to stay around that dollar amount.

When you are looking at a potential rental property you should bring a pen and a notebook with you to write down all the repair and updates necessary. Then you can add up an estimated cost for all the items on the list, this will be your budget if you are to purchase that property. If the property is listed for $35,000 and you have $20,000 in repairs on your budget, you might want to look for a better investment.

Don't Update Too Much

I always tell new investors, "Remember you are NOT going to be living here". Now it should be nice enough that you would be willing to live there but it would be a waste of money putting granite counters in a rental that you only get $700 a month in rent.

Every property and location are different. In some properties I have replaced the whole kitchen, changed layouts and even installed appliances and other properties I just carpet, paint and then rent.

You need to make all repairs needed to the property but when it comes to updates you have to decide what will be a good investment and what will give you a return on your investment.

Consider putting in a New Water Heater

There are a few items that are more cost effective to have done during the rehab then when you have a tenant occupying the property.

I just recently had to put in a new water heater in one of my rentals that was occupied. I got an estimate for $1,600 to have a plumber do the work. Now I was able to negotiate the price down and I save a few bucks by doing a little of the work myself, but the fact is that it cost me more because it was considered an emergency job.

If I would have put in a water heater when I was doing my rehab I could have saved a few hundred dollars because I had other plumbing work done and it would have cost less to do it all at once. I also don't like having to invest money into a property that is occupied. To be honest it was something I overlooked when I did my walkthrough of the property.

This brings me to my last point

Expect the Unexpected

Like I just mentioned, it is not likely that you will find everything that needs done when you do your walkthrough of the property. You could hire a home inspector and have a higher chance of catching everything but there are two reasons not to do that.

First, the seller won't give you as good of a deal if your put an inspection in the purchase agreement. Sellers love contracts with no contingencies like home inspections and they usually sell at a lower price just because there are no contingencies.

Second, the home inspector is not perfect. I see inspectors miss things all the time. That is why they carry Errors and Omissions Insurance.

I am not saying to not have an inspection, but I am saying you will get a better deal by not having it written into the contract. If you don't feel comfortable doing the inspection yourself, you could have an inspector look over the property before you write up the purchase agreement and that way you will know what you are getting into upfront.

How to Find a Good Tenant

When you start your rental business, you will find out that there are so many "bad" tenants but don't worry there are plenty of good tenants too you just have to find them. There are a few things you can do to help your chances of getting good tenants, the goal is to attract good tenants, so they come to you.

Location

You may be wondering why I didn't start with background and credit checks; don't worry I will get to that. I want to start with Location because this is where you will start your path to good investments and finding good tenants. Before you ever do a credit check you can help your chances of finding a good tenant by finding a good rental location.

Bad tenants like to stick together. If you purchase a property in an area that attracts bad tenants, then you will also attract bad tenants and you will have a hard time getting a good tenant interested in the property.

You may get an amazing deal in these locations, but it will not be worth it in the long run. It only takes one bad tenant to ruin your investment. You want to buy a property in a location that attracts good tenants.

Updates and Repairs

Every property you purchase should need to have some repairs and updating done, this is because you get a better deal on these properties.

You must make sure your properties are in good repair and have a few updates as well. Simple things like repainting and carpeting every five years helps. It all depends on how much rent you can get on each property but there are other updates you can do when you first purchase a property.

Occasionally I will do a kitchen and bath remodel on a property if I can get a return on it with a higher monthly rent. It is best to do all these types of rehab projects when you first buy the property, otherwise you will waste time having two big rehabs. It will save you time doing it all at once.

The more updates you have the better the tenants you can attract.

Set the Right Price

The idea is to set the price high enough but not too high. If you set the price too high your property will sit vacant until you finally find someone willing to pay your overpriced rent. It will be better in the long run to set it at market value and have very little vacant time.

Tenants will stay longer in a property that is priced correctly. Having a tenant stay for five or ten years produces more profit then having vacancies every year or two when your looking for new tenants.

You obviously do not want to set the price too low and just throw away profit every month. If you are struggling to figure out what market value would be, you can ask a Realtor, or you could call around to find out what other properties are renting for in that area.

Another thing to keep in mind is that the lower your monthly rent is the lower the quality of the tenants will be. Set your rent to maximize your profits and minimize your vacancies.

Background and Credit Check

This should be a no brainer. There are many options for background and credit check services. The one I use costs about $30 for the services I need. Its mostly hands off for me so I don't have to waste any time. I just put their name in and their email and they fill out their information and pay online.

My suggestion is to find a company that will handle everything online. You can even have the application process handled by these companies online. The more they do the less you do, and this is how you obtain passive income.

How to be a Successful Landlord

The most important aspect to be a good landlord is to take care of your properties. Don't run the property into the ground. Take care of your properties and they will take care of you.

Conduct Inspections

I like to schedule quarterly inspections on my occupied properties and weekly inspections on my vacant properties. I usually give my tenants about a two or three day notice. I don't want to just show up in case they are in the middle of something or they might not be home. You don't want to schedule it too far out though. If something strange is going on you need to know.

I have quarterly and end of lease inspection check lists on my website REinvestWise.com under the Resources tab in the Investors section.

Conducting routine inspections will ensure your property is in good repair and it will also encourage your tenants to take care of the property.

When I first started out, I had one rental and I didn't ever do any quarterly inspections. When the tenant decided to move out, I conducted an end of lease inspection and found that the clawfoot bathtub had a leak around the drain and it ruined the floor in the bathroom. I had to spend time and money fixing it after he moved. If I would have done quarterly inspections, I would have caught that sooner and I would have only needed to repair the leaky drain and not the entire floor. Inspections will be worth your time.

Keep Rent Current

Never ever allow a tenant to get behind on rent. It will only get worse. I have seen it happen dozens of times with other investors. It's like a snowball going downhill. Once it starts, they will just get farther and farther behind. As a rule of thumb once they are thirty days behind the deposit will cover it. If they miss a second payment you should start the eviction process because you will never see that money. I have never seen a tenant catch up from two months behind in rent.

I have a late payment penalty. I give them a 5-day grace period after the fifth day it is a $10 a day late fee. I make all rent payments due on the first of the month. If they pay on the sixth day of the month, they are late and owe a $50 late fee on top of the monthly rent payment. That's $10 per day starting on the first day after the due date of the first, so they were 5 days late.

If you have a long-term tenant that has been there for many years and they had something come up it wouldn't be out of the question to omit the late fee for the first time they are late. I find that tenants will respect you if you bend the rules for their benefit. Make sure you tell them that it will only be a one-time deal and next time they will have to pay the late fee. I have had success with this method.

Stick to the Lease

What ever the lease agreement says goes. It will be you and your tenant's rule book. Any time something comes up point back to the lease.

I have had tenants try to get a dog or wait until after they sign the lease to tell me they have a dog (even though I tell them upfront I have a no pet policy). I just point them back to the lease and tell them that it says, "NO PETS ALLOWED".

I have also had tenants try to move in extra people not listed on the lease. I make them write down all people that will be staying there on the rental application. I run background and credit checks on everyone over the age of 18. Then I put all names on the lease and those are the only people allowed to live there.

Stick to Your Plan

You should have short-term and long-term plans in place before you start investing in real estate. Make sure every property you buy, every rehab you do, every lease or purchase agreement you sign fits into your plan.

If a certain property is a killer deal but it will ruin your plan, then you should seriously consider passing on it. You might be able to pick up a good property but if it stalls out your plan or sets you back a year or two you may mess everything up.

Make a short-term and long-term plan and stick to them!

Chapter Four

Fix n' Flips

House flipping is a great career choice and real estate investing path. In my opinion the only downside of being a house flipper is that it is not truly passive income. With rentals you can build up your portfolio and one day down the road you can sit back and collect rent checks. With house flipping you must always be looking for a new flip and working on your current flip.

I don't want to scare you away with the negative, so I will now focus more on the positive.

As a house flipper you control your schedule, your income, your career and your life. Not everyone will make a great house flipper, but anyone can flip a house. This chapter will help you learn **How to Flip a House**, **How to Make Money Flipping Houses** and **Can You Become a House Flipper.**

By the end of this chapter you will know everything you need to know to become a successful house flipper.

1. **How to Flip a House**

Flipping a house seems like a simple thing, Buy a home, Fix it up then Sell it for a profit. It is not that easy. Many people have lost Thousands of Dollars trying to flip houses and failed, but I will help you become successful.

To simplify the process:

Obtain the funds to purchase a property

Purchase a property

Repair and update the property

Sell the property for a profit

It may look simple, but there are many details in each one of these steps. I will go over all of this in this chapter, so keep reading.

2. How to Make Money Flipping Houses

Not everyone that tries to flip houses makes money, becomes rich and gets their own tv show. There are plenty of people that lose money trying to flip houses and even successful house flippers lose money occasionally on a flip.

The idea is to play it safe on the first few. Don't try to hit a home run on your first swing, you just need to get on base. If you only make $2,000 on your first flip that's ok, actually that's great! You didn't lose any money and you can keep moving forward.

Here are the steps to making money flipping houses.

Find the Right Home

Just because a home is cheap it doesn't mean that it is the right home. Yes, you definitely need to find a property that is "Cheap" but there are so many other factors involved.

After Repair Value (ARV) is going to be the number one deciding factor on whether a property would be a good flip or not. You will need to calculate the cost to purchase, repair, hold and sell the property and then subtract that from the ARV, the difference will be your profit or loss.

In a perfect world the home you decide to flip will be "The worst home in the best neighborhood". You need to look for homes in areas that will be easy to resell. Areas with plenty of buyers looking to move into.

You can always find a really cheap home in a run-down area but even if you make the home beautiful you may not be able to find any buyers looking to move into that area.

Location is key!

Make Necessary Repairs and Update Wisely

You are probably buying a home that needs both repairs and updating. You will need to make all the repairs necessary to get the home to pass inspections.

If you plan on making money on this flip you will also need to update the home as well. You will need to make a budget before you buy the home. It is very important to have a budget and follow it. You will need to budget for updating the home. Don't forget to budget for the unexpected.

You need to be smart about what updates you are going with and how much they cost. You will also need to pay attention to what updates fit this home and location. For example, Granite counter tops may not be the right decision for a home in an $80,000 neighborhood.

Always try to put money into the items that increase a property's value, Flooring, Paint, Kitchens, Bathrooms, Decks, etc.

List the Home for the Right Price

There is nothing worse than putting a ton of time and energy into a house and then putting it on the market and watching it sit for months. If you did a great job remodeling, then the home should sell in just a matter of days in this current market.

The best way to achieve a quick sale at a great price is to hire a good local Realtor to list and sell your home. They will be able to price it correctly for you and most importantly they will market the home so that you will receive maximum exposure to buyers and possibly receive multiple offers.

When you make your budget make sure you put the costs to sell in it, Realtor Fees, commissions, holding costs, taxes and title fees.

3. Can You Become a House Flipper?

Everyone wants to become a house flipper right? Well, maybe not everyone does but if your reading this you must have thought about it. I want to help you decide if it's the right career choice for you.

Do You Have the Ability to Purchase a Property?

This does not mean that you have to have $300,000 in cash laying around, but if you do then you have a great head start.

You can fund the purchase in other ways then cash. Don't misunderstand me though, cash is the best option for house flipping but not the only option.

You can use equity loans and personal loans. If you have plenty of equity in your personal home, then you can just borrow against your home for the purchase and remodel of the flip. This is a great option due to the lower interest you pay on an equity line then other options.

You can use conventional loans to purchase investment properties. You need to remember that any time a bank is involved there will be limits to the condition of the home. Conventional loans are not too strict though.

You will pay a little higher interest with this option then an equity line and you will only get the money needed for the purchase and you will have to find money elsewhere to fund the remodel.

Some house flippers will use a combination of both equity and conventional loans, I have even seen people borrow against credit cards and be successful but in my opinion that is too risky with the high interest rates.

You can even use hard money loans, private lenders or financial backers but these options will really cut into your profits. They will come with higher interest rates and even take a percentage of your profits. I don't suggest these options for the beginning of your real estate investing career, after a few years and a dozen or so properties under your belt this may be an option you could use on occasion.

Do You Have Some Knowledge of the Construction and Remodeling Trades?

You cannot become a successful house flipper without having some knowledge of the repair and remodel side of the business. You don't need to be an expert in any trade, but you need to know what to look for and how things are fixed.

As long as you have some general knowledge of remodeling you will be ok but remember the less you know the more you will have to pay someone who does.

You could possibly partner with someone who knows the construction side better then you. Many house flippers are successful this way. If your better on the finances, then you handle that and let your partner handle the remodel.

Do You Have the Guts?

No matter how great a deal may seem there no guarantees when flipping a house. As with any investment there are risks involved.

You must have the guts to take the risk and buy your first property and flip it. Sometimes in the flipping business you will have to make a quick decision especially if a property is a great deal. This may make you extremely nervous, but you must be able to get through it and get the job done.

Anyone could be a house flipper but not everyone can be successful at it.

Chapter Five

Make a business Plan

There are many ways to create a successful real estate investing company. The main thing I want to stress isn't the actual plan but that you HAVE a plan. You will not be as successful as you can be if you don't have a plan. I'm not saying that you won't make any money, but it will be much harder to be profitable and you will never reach your full potential profit without a business plan.

You need to set yourself up for success and you need to prepare a clear path to successful real estate investing. The best way to do this is to create a business plan and follow it. You need to create this plan before you ever start looking at investment properties

Your FIRST Step to Real Estate Investing Is to Make A Business Plan!

I am going to focus on one format for a business plan that I think is the best for maximum growth and profit. This is the...

BRRRR Plan

This stands for **Buy, Renovate, Rent, Refinance, Repeat.**

This is the fastest way to build up a good portfolio quickly, unless you have a few hundred thousand dollars laying around.

1. **Buy a Property with Cash**

For this plan to work you need to start off with enough cash or equity to purchase your first property without a loan on it. The idea is to buy a property that needs repairs and updating.

2. Renovate the Property

After you buy the property then you will need to renovate it to make it worth more than you paid for it.

3. Rent the Property

After you have it renovated you will want to get it occupied quickly to start creating cash flow.

4. Refinance the Property

You will need to find a lender that will send out for a new appraisal. Most lenders will use your purchase price of the property as the value of the property. You can move forward this way, but you won't get very far. If you can't find a lender to work with you then you will have to wait one year from your purchase date for a traditional lender to send out for a new appraisal.

5. Repeat the Process

After you get your equity loan on the first investment property you will now want to use these funds to purchase your next property. Repeat the process over and over again.

The BRRRR plan may seem perfect, but this process isn't flawless though. At some point you will either get too small of an equity loan to purchase and renovate the next property or you may run into debt to income ratio issues.

As I just mentioned when you get the equity loan on the investment property you will need it to be enough to both purchase AND renovate the next property. Do not forget to budget the renovation before you purchase the property.

If you use the right lender, they will be able to use the rental income from each property as part of your income to boost your income enough to get you under the 45% debt to income ratio required from most lenders for investment properties.

This plan relies on using cash or an equity loan to start building your investment portfolio but there are other methods you can use that won't involve as much cash up front.

Conventional Loan Plan

This is just simply using conventional loans to purchase the investment properties. This plan makes it slightly hard to build up a portfolio because you will hit the debt to income ratio faster.

You will still need some cash upfront for the down payment and closing costs. When using conventional loans, you will have about $4,000 more in closing costs then when you purchase with cash. This means it costs more to purchase the property.

The benefit to using conventional loans is that you will have very low monthly payments on your investment properties. You will also have a structured payment plan that will allow you to pay off the loans in 20 years. You can plan your entire investing career around the payoff dates of the properties.

I know investors that will only use conventional loans when purchasing investment properties. I personally don't like conventional loan purchases because of the extra closing costs involved. You can get the seller to pay most of these for you, but chances are you will just be paying for it with a higher purchase price. This means that you have basically financed your closing costs and now you are paying interest on your closing costs.

No matter what plan you come up with and decide to go with there will be pros and cons to the plan. You will need to decide which plan is best for you and stick to it. For most people they won't have too many options as to which plan to use, sometimes their personal financial situation makes the decision for them.

Whether you have loads of cash on hand or not there will be a way to get started in real estate investing. I suggest talking to an experienced real estate investor for advice on your personal situation. Check out my Mentoring program on my website REinvestWise.com, the link to the mentoring page is **REinvestWise.com/mentoring-and-coaching** check it out and find a plan that works best for you.

Chapter Six

Why You Should Become a Realtor

Is Becoming a Realtor the Right Path for You?

Let's be honest being a Realtor is not for everyone. On my website REinvestWise.com I have a **"Questionnaire"** to help you determine if becoming a Realtor is the right career choice. The link to all the information you will need to become an agent is **REinvestWise.com/become-an-agent**

I want to point out some of the benefits of being a Realtor. This will also be helpful in making the decision, "Is being a Realtor right for me"?

Benefits of Being a Realtor

There are many benefits to being a Realtor, I won't go over all of them, but I will highlight a few benefits.

1. **Make Your Own Schedule**

This may be my favorite on this list! To have the ability to control your own schedule is amazing! I have the flexibility to schedule appointments and office hours when I need and want. I have not had to miss any of my kids' doctor's appointments, I did not need to use a vacation day or call off.

I have no need to worry about how many vacation days or sick days I have left. I am free to schedule a vacation whenever I want. If I wake up sick and can't go into work, I don't need to call a supervisor and try to get them to understand. I don't have to worry about how many "Points" I have left before I am fired.

With all that being said, obviously I can't be sick or go on vacation every day. With real estate the more you put into it the more you will get out of it or you could say the less you put into it the less you get out.

2. **You can Work from Home**

Actually, you can work anywhere, home, office, in the car, at the beach, etc. Anywhere you can bring your phone can be your work place for the day. You could pick up your phone while sitting on the couch and send an email or a text message to a client. I have negotiated deals on vacation more than once. I have emailed offers while watching a movie. I also have put hours of work in at my office, you literally can work anywhere. Now, your family may not appreciate you working during a movie or on vacation but, it can be done.

3. **Unlimited Income**

At most companies, like **"Nova Star Real Estate"** there is no commission cap. You can keep growing your income as much as you want. My company also has incentive programs where the more you sell the higher your commission percentage grows.

If you want to work real hard and close a deal every week or even every day you can. No one is stopping you. For every deal you close you receive a paycheck. Again, the more you put into it the more you will get out, so the more time you put into it the more money you will get. The sky is the limit.

4. Being a Realtor Gives you a Head Start on Real Estate Investing

If you are serious about real estate investing, then one of the best things you can do is get your real estate license. By being a Realtor, you gain insider information legally.

You can be one of the first to know when a property is on the market. You can find out if there are other offers on a property. You have access to the tools needed to find properties and determine their "Fair Market Value".

You can still be a successful real estate investor without being a Realtor IF you find a good Realtor to work with that knows the investing side of real estate, BUT you can eliminate the middle man by being the Realtor yourself.

Another great benefit of be a Realtor and a real estate investor is that you will get the commission on all the properties you purchase. You can not only pay for your license fees but also make a profit just from the properties you buy as investment properties.

I hope that I have intrigued you on the thought of being a Realtor. It really is a great career path and it can greatly benefit your real estate investing career. I hope that you have checked out the **"Should I Be a Realtor"** questionnaire. If you determine that you would like to become a Realtor or even if you just have questions, feel free to contact me.

Chapter Seven

Keep Moving Forward

You now have all the information you need to start making your business plan and start your real estate investing career. I talk to so many people that say they are interested in real estate investing. I have shown too many houses to potential investors that do not have the courage or boldness to pull the trigger.

Don't be one of those people!

You can do this!

Like I expressed in the very first chapter of this book **Anyone CAN Invest in Real Estate!!!**

You have done all the right things, you researched, you educated yourself and you can now build a business plan. You can start your career as a real estate investor now, but you can do one more thing to full proof your investments and ensure a more profitable career. I highly recommend that you take one extra step and find a mentor or a coach to work with you.

I have a mentoring program that will fit any budget. I have plans that give you unlimited access to an experienced mentor. Visit my website **REinvestWise.com/Resources** and visit the **Mentoring and Coaching** section for more information.

I can't stress to you enough the importance of starting out right. If you mess up on your first property you may never recover, or it may take years to just be able to start over. Don't take a huge risk on your first property. It is better to go with a property that will give you a small return and is a safer investment then to try and hit a home run and strike out.

Buying your first investment property is tough and its nerve racking but you can do it! It gets easier with every property you purchase. Your confidence will grow with every successful investment property that you add to your portfolio.

Your knowledge will grow as well. Every property you purchase will teach you something about real estate investing.

I want you to understand that building a real estate portfolio will take time. It will take years!!! Don't quit to early! It may be frustrating at first when you only have one property, and something breaks every month and you have to keep dumping money into it, but that's just part of the process. Don't let it overwhelm you.

Hopefully you followed my advice and repaired everything before you rented it out and this won't happen but sometimes things get missed and sometimes you can't see a potential problem during your rehab.

You may only be able to buy one property a year, but I want you to understand that its ok! Buying one property a year for 20 years will leave you in a great situation to sit back and take the checks to the bank. Sometimes you can build a portfolio much faster then 20 years. I have seen investors build a good portfolio in less then 10 years.

Don't get discouraged. Stay the course and

KEEP MOVING FORWARD!

www.ingramcontent.com/pod-product-compliance
Lightning Source LLC
Chambersburg PA
CBHW021513210526
45463CB00002B/1000